LAKE SUPERIOR RAILROAD.

LETTER

TO THE

HON. LEWIS CASS.

BY MORGAN L. DRAKE, ESQ.

PONTIAC.....MICHIGAN.

W. M. THOMPSON, BOOK AND JOB PRINTER.

1852.

LETTER.

Pontiac, November 19, 1852.

SIR :

It is proposed to solicit Congress at the ensuing session, for a grant of land to aid in constructing a Railroad route from Pontiac, in the State of Michigan, the present termination of the Detroit and Pontiac Railroad, by way of Flint, in Genessee County, to Marquette Bay in the County of Mason, and from Manitowoc on the opposite shore of Lake Michigan in Wisconsin, to Kewana Point on Lake Superior, with a branch to the Ontonagon, and a branch to Iron Bay and near the mouth of the Chocolate River. The distance may be thus stated, direct lines ;—

Detroit to Pontiac, now Railroad,	25 miles,
Pontiac to Marquette,	186,
Marquette across the Lake to Manitowoc,	60,
Manitowoc to Kewana Point,	196,
Branch to Iron Bay,	60,
Branch to Ontonagon,	40.

After leaving Flint, 31 miles from Pontiac, you strike the public lands, which continue to Marquette Bay, 155 miles. From Manitowoc to Green Bay, 37 miles, there is but little public lands. From Green Bay to Lake Superior, it is a wilderness, and all Government land, save so much as may have been taken in the Mining District. The object of going by the Flint is as follows, viz ; 1st, It will open up so much of a route to Saginaw Bay. 2d, It is the nearest point to the Government lands from Pontiac. 3d, It is about as direct a route as can be taken.

Congress has granted to Missouri, Illinois, Alabama and Mississippi, to aid in constructing Railroads, lands equal to six sections in width under the plea of opening the public domain. Though these lands, have not hitherto been sold for want of access to market, they are in the finest climate and are of the most generous soil in the Union. In the region to be opened by the Lake Superior route, it is directly the reverse. It is forbidding from the rigor of the climate, and the soil is not an inviting one to emigrants. Instead of fertile and level prairies, skirted with woods just sufficient to relieve the picture and to answer the wants of man, producing luxuriantly every desirable variety of agricultural products, like the land in the States named, this region is rough, rocky, mountainous, covered with a dense forest, and has the cold, hard, stiff soil common to higher latitudes. For these and other kindred reasons, it is thought Congress in that munificence which becomes the Government, would grant an additional section, say seven alternate sections on each side of the line. Indeed, twelve alternate sections on each side of the line will not be more than six in the States named.

By reference to the map it will be seen that Michigan is divided in such a manner as to prevent the citizens of the mineral region from mingling with those of the Peninsula, for seven months in the year, without traversing the wilderness through to Green Bay upon snow shoes, using the snow for a bed and the storm for a blanket. And it is of little avail that the citizens of that division are united to the Peninsula by the ties of government, so long as it is impracticable to extend and enforce over them the administration of the State for so great a portion of the year. In this connection it is worthy of remembrance that this state of things was forced upon Michigan by Congress, upon her admission into the Union, against her will, and upon the solicitation of Ohio, and through the votes of the older

States. Under these circumstances it would be but just and reasonable to expect, at least from the Ohio delegation, a generous and united support for this measure. That State, and the other States who combined with her upon the occasion alluded to, cannot upon principles of comity and fair, neighborly usage, now object to this grant of land in aid of establishing a communication on the only line that will answer the wants and meet the necessities of the two great divisions of our State, and thus enable us to overcome the barriers of nature and to say, in truth, "we are one people."

After the close of navigation the mails are taken only twice a month, and not sure at that, from Green Bay, through the forest, by two men who carry but a few pounds each. When the population shall increase, as it will, under the wonderful energy with which that country is now being improved, this public supply of the mail, which is all the Department can furnish under the present facilities for transporting it, and so insufficient for the transaction of business, will be a hardship difficult to endure.

The hardship will increase and keep pace with the improvement of the country, and must ever continue, unless some outlet of the kind contemplated is established. And this hardship will be experienced by the State as a body politic as well as by individuals.

With the setting in of the autumnal gales which sweep over Lake Superior with fearful violence, the navigation may be considered as closed. And it is found by dear bought experience, unsafe to depend upon obtaining supplies later than the middle of October, or earlier than the middle of May. Great expense and outlay is required to lay in suitable stores for eight months of winter imprisonment. And they are prevented from shipping their minerals and are compelled to heap them up as idle capital on the shores of the Lake to await the opening of navigation. Much difficulty is also found in employing laborers, as but few men are willing, without extra wages, to be debarred from all access to other portions of the Union, and virtually deprived of the enjoyments of the Post Office service for so great a portion of the year. In these several respects, Michigan is situated differently from any other State in the Union. By the proposed route supplies can be obtained, and the mineral sent forward to market summer and winter, and a daily mail would be secured to that country.—Lake Michigan between Marquette and Manitowoc is open on the average, and can be safely crossed from nine to ten months every year. This route will bring the Copper and Iron region within forty eight hours of Detroit and Chicago, and within four days of St. Louis and New York. It may be considered as an extension of the Illinois Central, the Michigan Southern, the New York and Erie, and the New York Central Railroads, as well as the Great Western Railroad through Canada. There is a road now being surveyed between Chicago and Milwaukie. The space between Milwaukie and Manitowoc, eighty miles, would be soon improved by a Railroad upon the construction of this route; and there would be a Rail road communication over the Illinois Central and its connections, twelve hundred miles to Mobile. This would give the entire valley of the Mississippi easy access to the Lake Superior country. Connecting with the Michigan Southern Railroad at Chicago, it would give access to the valley of the Ohio, and accommodate the travel around the head of Lake Erie to the upper country. Crossing the Lake and the Peninsula of Michigan, it would, at Detroit, connect with the road through Canada.

This route is wanted not by the State of Michigan only, but by other States. The seven States which encircle the American side of the western Lakes are commercially as much interested as Michigan. The States adjoining these, which pour their commerce through various channels upon these Lakes, and furnish powder, implements, machinery, laborers and merchandise to the Lake Superior region, are equally interested.

The various artizans of the Union who work in Iron and

Copper, owing to their superior properties, seek these materials with great avidity from Lake Superior, and they are equally interested with Michigan. The Iron mines are being wrought principally by the capital of Ohio, Pennsylvania and Massachusetts. The capital of Ohio, Pennsylvania, New York, Connecticut, Massachusetts and the District of Columbia, as well as other sections of the Union is liberally invested in the development of the Copper Mines. The Southern States will supply that country over the Illinois Central Road with sugar and tobacco, two important items in supplying a mining population. Illinois and the valley of the Mississippi will supply the corn and pork, and Wisconsin the flour and other agricultural products.

Aside from the purposes of government, and the mere unfolding of its mineral wealth, a wealth which will in a few years become the pride of the nation, other States are far more interested in this measure than the Peninsula of Michigan. It is not then merely local selfishness on the part of Michigan and Wisconsin in asking for a grant of land to aid in constructing this route. The interest in the mines now being worked, held in New England, is valued at millions, while there is not a dollar invested in them from Wisconsin. The amount of capital invested in them in Ohio is more than that from Michigan. That from New York will exceed that of Michigan a thousand fold. And that from Pennsylvania is nearly equal to all the rest. This is not then a project of mere local interest, and cannot be objected to on that ground. It is a matter which concerns the Atlantic states as well as ours. It will bind the extreme north to the south, and add another bond to the perpetuity of the Union.

We have seen that these mines have so far been wrought under obstacles of no ordinary character. By examining the statistics it will appear that they have been improved to a surprising extent, so much so as to render it difficult to compute how far it would enhance the value of the whole mineral region, by thus increasing the facilities of access to it, or to appreciate the enthusiasm with which those now in that region would hail the establishment of such an outlet, or estimate the increased rapidity in which the mines would be developed, or count the great saving of time and money in opening and working the mines so as to render them a source of profit.

The lands along this route are worthless to the Government and the people,—without some improvement of the kind, they will long remain in an unbroken wilderness. But once construct this road, the government lands would be eagerly sought for, and there would be numerous flourishing settlements along the route—the germs of the settlement of the adjoining country. Hither would gather foreign emigrants, as well as enterprising Americans—furnishing at once, the source for the settlement of the lands--for laborers to construct the road--and for hands to be employed in the mines.

Of the lands which Congress granted to the State of Illinois, for the construction of the Illinois Central Railroad and Branches, 428,554 acres in the Kaskaskia and Shawnut districts had been in market thirty years; 344,672 acres had been in market twenty two years in the Vandalia district; 372,702 acres had been in market in the Dansville district nineteen years, and 465,948 acres had been in market eleven years in the Dixon district. There is now through the influence of this road an effective demand for these lands, and the reserved sections are reported to be selling by Government at prices varying from $2,50 to $7,00 per acre, and on the average at $5.00 per acre. And it is stated in the public Journals that the Government will sell the reserved sections at a profit of about $9,000,000 over the usual government price. If the rich prairie lands of Illinois remained for twenty or thirty years unsold for want of access to market, it may be said the lands on this route will not sell for ages. Though we may not expect they would sell at as great an advanced price as the Illinois lands, it is manifest Government would be largely profited by making the grant and thus securing the construction of the road. There cannot then be any objection to this grant upon the score of loss to the Government. It will cost the Government nothing. It will be like casting bread upon the waters that it may return again with a blessing. This is one of the highest, most noble of the offices of the Government; giving to increase, not to impoverish.

It is too late in the history of Cougressional legislation to object to these grants on the score of precedent. The precedent was, as you are aware, established in the administration of Gen. Washington, to open a road through the then North west territory. It was repeated for like purposes on several occasions in the subsequent administrations, and has been more recently enforced by grants to four different States. And the precedent has proved to be a good one. It works no evil, no harm to any, but it does good; good to the people, to the state, to the nation. Such is the result of experience.

The only question which can well be raised is whether the object to be attained is of sufficient importance to demand the attention of the National Legislature, and it is deemed further remarks unnecessary on this point. In its character, it is national; it will open a public highway thro' the public domain to a distant and almost inaccessible portion of the Union, in the bosom of which lies unavailable, numerous, vast, rich mines of Iron and Copper, two valuable items in the column of a nation's wealth; mines unsurpassed in purity and value—unequaled by any thing of the kind in the basin of the Atlantic.

It is difficult to see how the generous mind can object to this appropriation. It cannot be objected to for want of

precedent, for that is established; nor for the want of general utility, for of that there can be no doubt; nor upon the ground of any cost or loss to the government, for experience proves it will be a source of profit.

Government stretches forth an arm over the sea, and sends her fleets to the remotest corners of the earth, in behalf of the commercial business of the country, and opens new avenues of commerce,—and why not stretch forth an arm over the wilderness, to open avenues whereby the agricultural and industrial business of the country may join themselves in closeer bonds with commerce, and thus extend the interest of both. The business of the country, upon the land and upon the ocean, must govern the nation. The business of the world must govern the world; and the sooner we, as a people, unconditionally, unreservedly surrender and yield obedience to this principle, the more the highest interests and true prosperity of the country will be promoted.

There is a special reason why this measure should be pressed upon the consideration of Congress at the ensuing session. The sentiment seems to prevail that the public lands are no longer to be husbanded as a source of revenue. In accordance with this sentiment, a bill was, at the last session of Congress, introduced into the House of Representatives, and passed the House, and is now in the Senate, and will come up for consideration as unfinished business, known as the Bennett Bill, for the distribution of 60,000,000 of acres of public lands among the several States—to each State in the ratio of her representation in Congress. These lands are to be granted to the old States for the purposes of education, and to the new States for internal improvement. It provides that such Railroad grants as are passed during the session that that bill is passed, shall be deducted from the lands to be donated by that bill.

This measure is highly favored by the old States.—Should it become a law, the land donated to the new States will be subject to be specially appropriated by the respective Legislatures. Experience in Western State legislation proves, or at least gives much reason to fear, that if this bill should pass, the lands will, in the scramble, be frittered away. Every township will want an appropriation. Every member will have a favorite object, and the lands will be devoted to minor objects, and the construction of no great, important national work, will be secured. But let Congress make the grant in a separate bill, or by amendment to that bill, appropriating lands to this particular object, and no other—the ultimate construction of the work will be secured—and there can be no question but that its construction will be hastened by such a grant. This course will do no injury to the State or the Nation. No more lands will be appropriated to the new States than will be given by the Bennett Bill. Wisdom dictates the lands should be appropriated, if at all, to objects of general, national utility. In so doing, the interest of the States, new and old, will be promoted, and no one injured. Respectfully, your ob't serv't,

MORGAN L. DRAKE.

Hon. Lewis Cass.

(COPY.)

A BILL making a grant of land to the States of Michigan and Wisconsin in aid of the con struction of a Rail Road line from Pontiac to Lake Superior.

SECTION 1. Be it enacted by the Senate and House of Representatives of the Unite States in Congress assembled, That there be and is hereby granted to the States of Mich igan and Wisconsin respectively, for the purpose of aiding in making a railroad fro Pontiac, in the State of Michigan, by the way of the Town of Flint, to a point at or ne the shore of Lake Michigan, in the county of Mason in said state, and from a point a or near the shore of said lake, in the county of Manitowoc, in the State of Wisconsin, t a point to be selected upon Kewana Point, at or near the shore of Lake Superior, with branch to some point at or near the mouth of the Ontonagon River; and also a branch t some point at or near Iron Bay upon Lake Superior, every alternate section of land des ignated by odd numbers, for seven sections in width on each side of said road and bran ches; But in case it shall appear that the United States have, when the line or route o said road and branches is definitely fixed, sold any section or part of any section hereb granted, or that the right of pre-emption has attached to the same, then it shall be lawfu for any agent or agents, to be appointed by the Governor of the said respective states, t select from the lands of the United States most contiguous to the lands which may hav been sold, or to which the right of pre-emption may have attached as aforesaid, so much land in alternate sections or part of sections on the route of said road and branches, a shall be equal to such lands as the United States have sold or to which the right of pre emption may have attached, which lands being equal in quantity to every alternate sec tion for seven sections in width, on each side of said road and branches for the whole length thereof, the said respective states within their several and respective jurisdiction shall have and hold and may dispose of for the uses and purposes aforesaid: *Provide* That the lands to be so located shall in no case be further than fifteen miles from the line of the said road, or branches, as the case may be: *And Provided* That the lands hereby granted shall be applied in the construction of said road and branches respectively, in quantities corresponding with the grant for each, by the respective states, and within their several and respective jurisdictions; And that said road from Manitowoc to Ke wana Point, shall be made in a continuous line: *And Provided further*, That it shall be competent to alter and re-locate any portion of the line of said road and branches, if necessary to its economical construction, but not so as to materially change the route.

SEC. 2.—And be it further enacted, that a copy of the survey of said road and branch-es, shall be forwarded to the proper local land offices respectively, and to the General Land Office in Washington City, within ninety days after the completion of the same.

SEC. 3.—And be it further enacted, that the sections and parts of sections, which by such grant shall remain to the United States, within seven miles on each side of said road, and branches, shall not be sold for less than double the minimum price of the pub-lic lands when sold; which lands shall from time to time be offered at public sale, to the highest bidder, under the direction of the Secretary of the Interior; and shall not be sub-ject to entry until they shall have been so offered at public sale

SEC. 4,—And be it further enacted, that the said lands hereby granted to the said re-spective States, shall be subject to the disposal of the respective legislatures thereof, so far as the same shall be within the boundaries of the said states respectively, for the pur-poses aforesaid, and no other. And the said rail road and branches shall remain a pub-lic highway, for the use of the Government of the United States, free from toll or any other charge for the transportation of any property or troops of the United States.

SEC. 5.—And be it further enacted, that the said lands shall not be disposed of, or sold, otherwise than in trust for the purposes aforesaid, faster than the construction of said road shall progress. And as to so much of said road and branches as shall not be con-structed within fifteen years from the passage of this act, the said respective states shall take nothing by this grant, and the title to said lands hereby granted, for the unfinished portion of said road and branches, shall reinvest in the United States, to have and hold the same, in the same manner as if this act had not been passed.

SEC 6.—And be it further enacted, that the United States Mail shall be at all times transported on said railroad and branches, under the direction of the Post Office depart-ment, at such price as Congress shall by law direct, unless the authorities having control of said road, can otherwise agree.

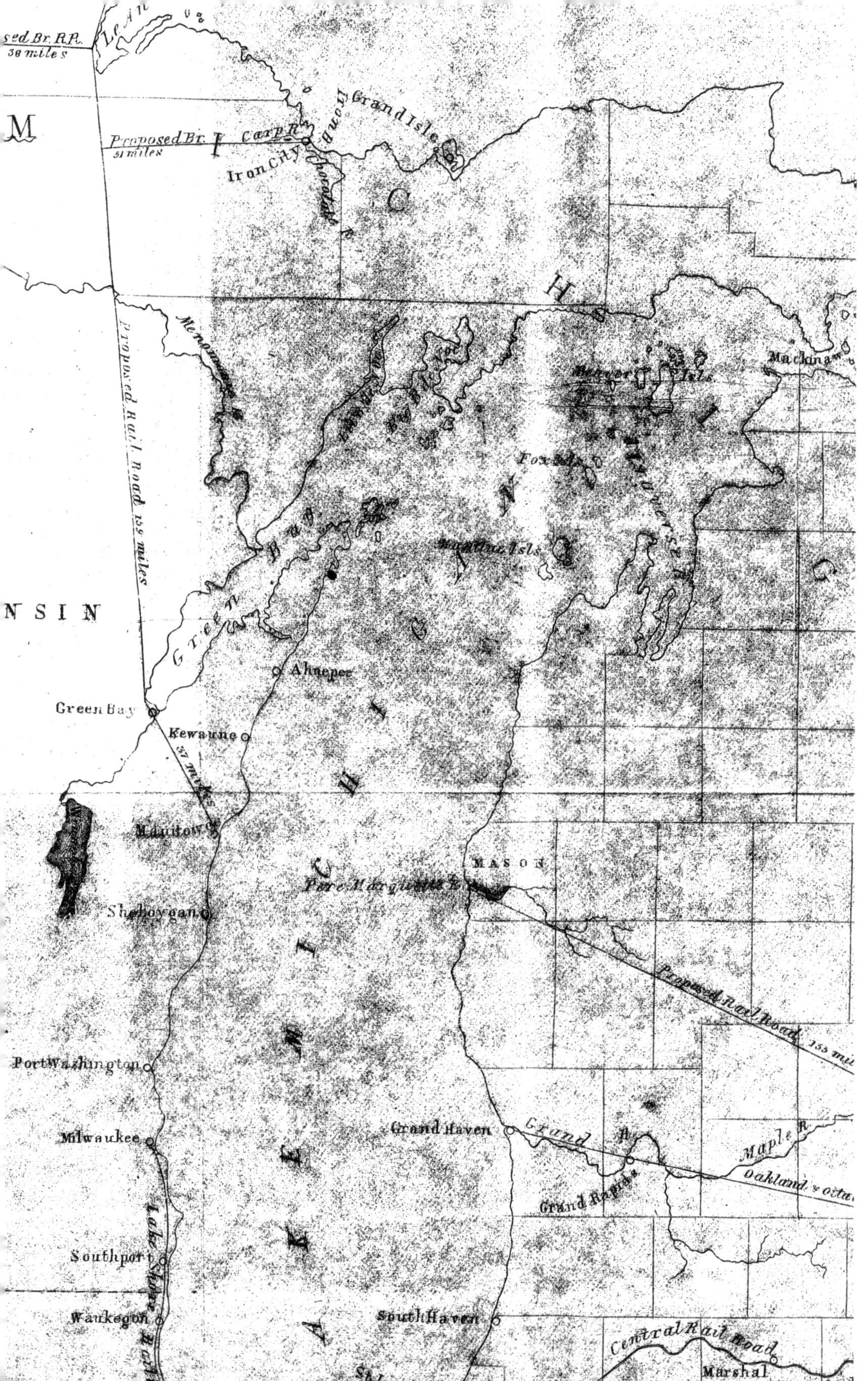

sed Br. R.R.
38 miles
Proposed Br.
51 miles
Carp R.
Iron City
Grand Isle
Chocolate R.
Menominee R.
Proposed Rail Road 159 miles
Beaver Isls.
Mackinaw
Fox Isls.
Manitou Isls.
Green Bay
Ahnepee
Kewaunee
57 miles
Manitowoc
MASON
Pere Marquette R.
Sheboygan
Proposed Rail Road
153 mil
Port Washington
Milwaukee
Grand Haven
Grand R.
Grand Rapids
Maple R.
Oakland & Otta
Lake Shore R.
Southport
Waukegan
South Haven
Central Rail Road
Marshal
NSIN

www.ingramcontent.com/pod-product-compliance
Lightning Source LLC
LaVergne TN
LVHW020640110826
845149LV00004B/1296

* 9 7 8 1 4 1 8 1 8 9 7 6 1 *